THE DRUMME

and other poems o

by

Roy Packer

Published by Roydon Books, Ottery St. Mary 1993

My thanks to the following:

The 'Express & Echo', Exeter, for permission to use their photographs of Littleham Church, Orcombe Point and the tar barrel rolling.

Helen Sear, Keith Bowden and Bill Packer for other photographic work.

The National Maritime Museum, London, and the Ashworth Gallery, University of Manchester, for the granting of reproduction rights where mentioned.

Dear "Pip" for the cover and map.

Printed by South West Typesetting Service, Sidmouth.
Tel.: (0395) 513622

ISBN 0 9519947 0 0
Price £5.95

CONTENTS

THE DRUMMER'S STONE

Offwell is a pleasant village lying off the Honiton to Axminster road. In the Offwell Parish Register a burial is recorded as follows: 'Unknown youth. July 11th, 1701.'

Captain J. R. W. Coxhead, who wrote articles and books about East Devon, tells, in his 'Legends of Devon', published in 1954, of a legend which was handed down in the family of Copleston of Offwell for many generations. The details were passed to him by Commander R. Copleston, R.N., on November 5th, 1950.

He was told that the burial entry referred to a drummer boy who met with a sad fate.

On the A35 heading towards Axminster from Honiton there is a cross-roads leading to Offwell on the right and the village of Cotleigh on the left. In olden times it was known as Cotleigh Cross but became known as 'Drummer's Stone'. It is not far from, and the first cross-roads after, the Windmill Garage.

There is no stone nearby but about 50 yards to the north of the cross-ways there was a stone, an old boundary stone, broken up by a gardener in the early 1920's to make a rockery. It was on that stone that the unknown youth was alleged to have been strangled.

There are old people in the area who remember 'Drummer's Stone' as a bus-stop designation.

THE DRUMMER'S STONE

He'd been at sea for three long years,
Yet still was just a lad;
He'd left his home with sobs and tears,
He'd made his mother sad.
Determined, he had gone to sea,
For he must see beyond
The Church, the ivied Rectory,
The green, the village pond.

He'd found it hard, he'd found it tough,
He'd hated most of all
Those shipmates who were crude and rough,
And most were strong and tall;
For he was but a little lad,
Although his jaw stuck out.
Quite soon he learned the rat-tat-tat,
He threw the sticks about.

A natural drummer boy, they said,
Who struck a brisk tattoo,
With rhythm from his toes to head,
He knew just what to do
By instinct. Though his heart was sad,
His beats were brave and strong,
His stirring rolls made others glad:
His sticks could sing a song.

He dreamt of home in hammock slung,
His mother then seemed near;
And when he woke sobs sometimes wrung
His tiny frame, and fear
Possessed him as the vessel swayed
And dipped upon the sea.
Would he see home again? Afraid,
He felt it would not be.

And in the Navy three years passed,
'Til he was given leave
From Plymouth Sound. He thought at last
It could be he'd achieve
His wish to be at home again
To see his mother dear;
He would walk there through mist and rain
To try to bring her cheer.

They had been poor and she had slaved
To raise her family;
The drummer boy for three years saved
His pay, for he could see
The sacrifices that he made
Might leaven her hard life,
And though he was but poorly paid,
Could soften years of strife.

He stitched the money in his belt,
He would not spend a groat.
His little fortune would not melt
Concealed beneath his coat.
His home in Devon to the East
Was sixty miles away,
But he would starve until the feast
When home he'd found his way.

A shipmate saw him plying thread,
And glimpsed the money store;
He tailed him with a stealthy tread
When they had gone ashore.
When city streets were left behind
He shouted loud, "Ahoy,
I'm on this road, if you don't mind,
I'll join you, drummer boy."

The drummer boy was sore afraid,
He didn't like this lad:
For he pursued a filthy trade.
He knew that he was bad.
But he was strong and he was tall,
What could be say but "Yes"?
Around his waist he held his all.
He walked on in distress.

He would not stop, he'd wear him out
By sheer tenacity.
He plodded on, his heart was stout,
He'd fight mendacity.
He would not sleep, he would not rest,
He'd conquer every hill.
He took deep breaths upon each crest:
The drummer boy had will.

He walked and walked all through the night,
The shipmate plodded too.
There were no words, although afright,
He knew what he must do:
He must not flag, he must not fail,
His tired limbs must thrust,
He must keep on and never quail.
He brooded on the dust.

For dust is us and what we were
In aeons long ago:
The drummer boy saw all things clear
Upon that walk of woe.
And dawn had brought another day,
This day the sun shone clear:
His village was not far away,
Come joy, the end of fear.

Offwell Parish Church

At Cotleigh Cross the poor boy swayed
And sank down on the stone:
Exhausted, yet not now afraid
Although they were alone.
For now he saw his mother's face,
He felt her presence near:
He'd won the frantic, nightmare race,
He'd seen the end of fear.

His strangled body soon was found
By one who walked that way;
His scattered clothes were on the ground,
No signs of any fray.
Now near three hundred years have passed,
Though why, not often known,
The crossway, where he breathed his last,
Is called "The Drummer's Stone."

GHOSTS OF THE WARREN

'Memorials of Exmouth' were compiled by the Reverend William Everitt, M.A., and from them I gleaned the facts for this narrative poem. He said that hundreds went out to the cliffs of Orcombe to look at the battle which he described as an 'unwanted sight' for among those who watched were parents and relatives of members of the English crew.

The Reverend William Everitt said that the only one of the English crew killed, William Bence, had, when his book was published in 1885, relatives still living in Exmouth and Budleigh Salterton. He also took an extract from an indenture dated 1847 which ran thus: 'The said William Bence was killed in an engagement off Beer, on board the ship Defiance, on or about the year 1782, and was buried in the churchyard of Littleham.' The register of his burial was dated June 14th, 1782.

Lieutenant Cadman, the commander of the English ship, received rapid promotion, for two years later, as Captain Cadman, he commanded the Helena sloop of war, which, lying in Torbay, was instrumental in recapturing men who had escaped from a convict ship.

It is likely that the action between the Dutch and English privateers in that June of 1782 revived, certainly in East Devon, patriotic pride which was at a low ebb for it then seemed certain that the American colonies were winning their independence.

The Reverend William Everitt wrote: 'The slain Dutchmen were buried on the Warren, which the superstitious long believed to have been haunted by their spirits.'

GHOSTS OF THE WARREN

Have the ghosts of the Dutchmen departed,
Have they left the Warren at last?
Have they gone back home to the Zuyder Zee,
Have they found their way across the sea,
Back to the Low Countree?

Twenty-one Dutchmen were buried there,
Buried in sand one grave to share;
Pitched in stiff to a piper's tune,
While the sun blazed down on a day in June,
After a victory.

The 'Zeuze' of Flushing, a privateer,
Launched but three weeks with a rousing cheer,
With a hundred men aboard and more,
Was standing off the Dorset shore,
Seeing what she could see.

The little 'Defiant' with guns so few
Decided to spoil the Dutchmen's view,
And off West Bay she set her rig
To bear down fast on the foreign brig,
Helped by an Easterly.

She got in fast with some telling blows,
The 'Zeuze' set her sails with a bloodied nose
And headed West across Lyme Bay;
Her big guns boomed as she sailed away,
'Defiant' on her lee.

The Dutchmen fought hard but their ship was new,
The guns were strange to the fresh-formed crew:
They aimed too high while 'Defiant's' men
Hit their big hull again and again
As she laboured through the sea.

At Exmouth there was holiday,
The sun shone bright throughout that day,
And people strolled along the shore,
With thoughts removed from waging war,
But that was not to be.

On Orcombe Point they saw them first,
They heard the guns, they thought the worst:
'Defiant' now had rigging torn,
Her sails bedraggled and forlorn.
'Twas not a victory.

Orcombe Point

The small 'Defiant' they all knew,
Two Exmouth men were in her crew.
Then, as the Dutch ship passed the head
They saw its wounded and its dead
Laid out for all to see.

And then they heard above the din
The merry pipe of William Flynn
From Exmouth, with his jolly jig
Triumphant as they chased the brig
Across the Devon sea.

They saw the 'Zeuze' was holed and slow,
Her timbers splintered down below;
And as 'Defiant' closed in fast,
The Dutch colours lowered on her mast;
It was a victory

To Exmouth Harbour came the prize,
With loud huzzas and shining eyes
The crowd who'd watched the thrilling fight
Pressed closer to the gruesome sight
Now tied up at the quay.

Lieutenant Cadman and his crew
Were heroes cheered though well they knew
That God, or fate, or luck had seen
Them safely berthed, for there had been
One lonely casualty.

The one man killed was William Bence
Of Exmouth, and in recompense
He had a funeral that was grand
At Littleham, though 'twas inland,
Not too far from the sea.

Aboard the 'Zeuze' were blood and bones
New-shattered, and the fevered groans
Of wounded men who knew full well
Their living meant a prison cell
And years of misery.

And in the crimson lake there lay
The corpses who had breathed that day:
They now with strange, bright-staring eyes
Embraced the vastness of the skies
In their eternity.

The skipper of the 'Zeuze' looked old,
The day was hot, his heart was cold;
That dawn so full of promise bright
Had brought the longest day of night
That he would ever see.

Have the ghosts of the Dutchmen departed
From Dawlish across the strait?
They moaned at night for years and years,
They formed will o' wisps from their frozen tears,
Missing the Low Countree.

Littleham Church where William Bence was laid to rest in the Churchyard

ST. SAVIOUR'S BRIDGE

Ottery St. Mary was described by the Reverend Richard Polwhele in his History of Devonshire, published in 1797, as 'long a place of eminence.'

Its glorious Church, similar with twin transeptal towers, to the great Cathedral Church of St. Peter in Exeter, was rebuilt as a collegiate church during the inspirational Bishopric of Grandisson. The Church of St. Mary at Ottery still has its squat spire on the North tower. Exeter Cathedral had one similarly sited, as can be seen on Hoker's pictorial Map of Exeter of 1587, but it was removed in 1752 as being unsafe. Ottery's spire, too, was unsafe, and the worshippers there were in some danger until the early years of this century when it was rebuilt. It has again received recent renovation.

Apart from being an important market town, surrounded by fertility, Ottery St. Mary was noted for its ecclesiastical significance.

Yet the town's greatest fame now derives from having been the birthplace of the genius, Samuel Taylor Coleridge.

The story of the Coleridges may be read elsewhere, but suffice it to say that in the late eighteenth century a clever father, with no worldly aspirations, coupled to an ambitious wife, produced a remarkable and diversified family who achieved much in this world.

The youngest son, the poet, was then considered the failure. An older brother, James, who reached the rank of Colonel in the Army, married money and fathered a line which contained eminent lawyers. His grandson, Lord Chief Justice of England, became the first Lord Coleridge. His seat was, and still is lived in, by the present Lord Coleridge, in Ottery St. Mary.

In September, 1987, Lord Coleridge, Q.C., gave a lecture entitled 'The History of the Town of Ottery St. Mary'. It was delivered in the Church Institute in Yonder Street, a building still in active use near the centre of the town.

He spoke of 'the chapel of St. Saviour, which gave its name to St. Saviour's Bridge, then a stone arched bridge, containing on the depths of one of its piers a small altar, with sacred flame alight.'

Complaining bitterly about the useful, but hideous structure which had replaced it, he prayed that this, too, might be swept away by the turbulent River Otter.

ST. SAVIOUR'S BRIDGE

It's said a sacred flame burned there,
In centuries ago.
It flickered in the keen night air
Above the Otter's flow.
Inside a pier, an altar stood,
Gave blessing to the span
Which bridged the never-ceasing flood,
A crossing made by man.
Yet God was thanked, for flame was lit,
And tended carefully;
And through the stonework's narrow slit
It burned for all to see.

St. Saviour's Bridge was truly blessed,
And sturdily stood fast;
Its arches had withstood the test
Of time, until at last
The Otter boiled, the flame blew out,
An altar dark was new:
The torrent raged, and all about
Was chaos as it grew
Upon dulled brains the knowledge that
The bridge was swept away.
And Exeter without that bridge,
Was very far away.

It was a dark December night
When waters, never tame,
Saw to the dowsing of that light,
The final, sacred flame.
The hump-backed bridge had gone for good,
Come morning, plain to see,
Its arches then forever would
Be but a memory.
And in the swirling, frothy flow,
The masoned stones were free.
The Otter made them pebbles now
To push them to the sea.

St. Saviour's Bridge undergoing strengthening and widening in 1992

But man must live and man must fight
To feed a family.
The damage done on that dark night
Required a remedy.
The Otter must be tamed again
For men to earn their bread,
And though it never ceased to rain,
A bridge must go ahead.
And what about the sacred flame?
On this there was accord,
The bridge must bear St. Saviour's name
In honour of the Lord.

They thought it wise to shift its site,
To change the Exon road;
This bridge must last, but was it right
If just one span bestrode
The stream? For there could never be
A chapel with a flame,
An altar tended patiently:
Things could not be the same.
And then in 1849,
It was the iron age;
An iron bridge, that would be fine.
So let the torrents rage!

The bridge was built, some hearts were sad
To see a stark new bridge.
The road was wide, some folks were glad,
But not Lord Coleridge.
He longed for such a flood as would
Sweep ugly change away.
It did not come, the bridge has stood
Until the present day.
But now the road no longer wide
For modern traffic's flow:
For sometimes lorries hit its side.
The bridge, some thought, must go.

Yet that old bridge, once hideous,
Was now our heritage;
It was thought wrong, invidious,
To turn our history's page.
The eyesore now was beauty,
For many years had passed,
So it was clearly duty
To make the old bridge last.
And yet the sacred flame has gone —
No chapel with a light.
No flame to burn perpetually,
However wild the night.

*The plaque on the wall of the Churchyard which commemorates
Samuel Taylor Coleridge*

THE BALLAD OF BITTERY CROSS

Escot is a location, but a few miles from Ottery St. Mary, yet remote from it, for the two are divided by the constant traffic of the A30.

The nearest village to Escot is Talaton. Escot was the home of the lord-of-the manor of Ottery St. Mary. Sir Walter Yonge commenced the building of a fine house there after he bought the Escot estate in 1680. It was not completed until after the 'Glorious Revolution' of 1688.

Although, like most of the gentry, eschewing the cause of the Duke of Monmouth, Sir Walter was active in his support of William of Orange. John Locke, 'that most modern and reasonable of philosophers', was, after exile in France and Holland, one of the entourage of Willam and Mary. He obviously struck up a friendship with Sir Walter Yonge for he visited Escot. Tradition has it that he was responsible for the pattern of some of the tree-planting in the park.

The park is still beautiful, but, alas, the old house has gone, burnt to the ground in a fire on the 28th December, 1808. By that time the Yonges had left, for Sir George Yonge who, as Secretary of State for War, had entertained George III and his family at Escot in 1789, indulged in an ill-fated industrial experiment which required money. He sold the estate, and also the lordship-of-the-manor to Sir John Kennaway in 1794.

After the fire, the first stone of the new house was laid by an infant, John Henry Kennaway, on the 6th September, 1837. He was to prove a grat benefactor to Sidmouth and Ottery St. Mary, and a conscientious representative in Parliament.

There is a mysterious atmosphere at Escot, now largely dispelled by an imaginative aquatic centre conceived by one of the younger Kennaways. It is a place of tranquillity in contrast to the main road not far away.

William Makepeace Thackeray, the Victorian novelist, sensed the melancholy of Escot. He, as a young boy, stayed at Larkbeare, rented from the Kennaways, half a mile away, and in 'Pendennis' he wrote of 'the carp-pond in Clavering Park, a dreary pool with

Bittery Cross in the August of 1992

innumerable whispering rushes and green elders, where a milkmaid drowned herself in the Baronet's grandfather's time, and the ghost was said to walk still.'

Clavering Park was clearly Escot.

Possibly the memory of corpses, free-swinging in the wind on a height above Escot, had a persuasive influence over the centuries.

Their sad story is told in a poem written in ballad form.

THE BALLAD OF BITTERY CROSS

They called the crossroads Bittery,
A sad, bleak name of woe;
A place of human misery,
Of suffering long ago.

Their bodies hung on gibbets high,
And rotted for a year:
They stood out stark against the sky,
To cast their shade of fear.

Those men were hanged and there displayed,
A message clear to all:
A cruel example had been made,
A lesson to appal.

Sir Walter Yonge, the manor's lord,
Looked at those whitening bones,
He also plainly heard the word,
The darker undertones.

For he had entertained the Duke,
His sympathies were clear;
Those hangings were a harsh rebuke
That he must always fear.

At Escot they had worked for him
To build his fine abode;
It grieved him that a fate so grim,
Had met them on that road.

Sir Walter, like his men, was sad
When Catholic James was king:
To serve the Pope was surely bad,
A very wicked thing.

Escot House

And then the gladsome news came through
That Monmouth had returned.
A Protestant he was, they knew,
He was at Lyme, they learned.

The building workers downed their tools
To join the rebel cause.
Sir Walter, sadly, thought them fools
To break the country's laws.

For he knew well they would be caught:
The Duke, though fair of face,
Was quite unfitted, so he thought,
To rule an island race.

And after many a day and night
Of fears and suffering,
They fought a desperate, hopeless fight,
And James was still their king.

Near Sedgemoor, Weston Zoyland Church
Became their fetid cell;
They moaned, half-starved, no room to move,
That House of God was Hell.

When, broken men, they swayed in chains
Before Judge Jeffrey's bench,
They could not know that their remains
Would cause a nauseous stench.

A stench at Talaton, their home,
A name with poignant ring,
Where air was sweet, and there was love,
And daffodils in Spring.

They hung them there for all to see;
To nature they were meat.
On gibbets like Iscariot's tree,
They typified defeat.

They called the crossroads Bittery,
A sad, bleak name of woe;
A place of human misery,
Of suffering long ago.

THE TUMBLING WEIR

Mention was made, in the introductory notes to the previous poem, 'The Ballad of Bittery Cross', of the participation by Sir George Yonge in an industrial experiment. This was the building of a cloth factory in Ottery St. Mary, allied to the re-building and modernisation of the existing corn mill.

Sir George spent £40,000 on the project, which was a vast sum then. Some of his investment was probably spend on the 'Tumbling Weir'.

Today the factory, much extended, is occupied by Ottermill Switchgear.

Sir George and his wife spent their declining years in 'grace and favour' apartments in Hampton Court Palace.

THE TUMBLING WEIR

The River Otter long ago
Possessed a wild, erratic flow:
It tore down bridges, broke its banks,
And played a lot of irksome pranks.
The Saxons used the busy bourne
And used its force to grind their corn.
To drive their stones they cut a leat:
In olden times no easy feat.
The old mill gave the town its bread
For centuries, or so it's said.

And then, in 1788,
Or near enough that long-passed date,
A grand new plan was set on course,
And water had to be the source
Of power. James Watt and his steam
Were, at that time, a kettle dream.
New flour and grist mills there would be,
And close by a factory
To make stout cloth, to bring renown
And welcome work to Ottery town.

The engineers had done their stuff:
The millstream was not wide enough,
They thought, to give sufficient thrust.
They drew their plans, they had to trust
Their own experience. The wheel,
A very large one, had to feel
A mighty force, a pent up surge
Of rushing waters which would urge
The frames to weave, the stones to grind
Unceasingly, to aid mankind.

The Mill-stream and the Tumbling Weir

Yet there were dangers in their schemes,
For they were bold, and grandiose dreams
Are fraught with peril. If they made
The millstream wider, then they laid
A trap for flooding of the works:
('They knew the Otter's wilder quirks).
A path for excess water must be found;
It could, they thought, pass underground
To feed the Otter down below,
And aid the great wheel's steady flow.

The ironmasters then were called.
They listened to the scheme, enthralled.
They scratched their heads, and thought, and thought,
Then said at last, "It didn't ought
To be beyond our skills. Your wheeze
Is good, and with the weir you'll squeeze
Great power with safety. 'Twill be fun
To make it. Yes, it can be done."
The mill stream widened, they were sure
The project's future was secure.

And so they built the fantasy,
The tumbling weir. It's there to see.
It is unique in history's lore,
Or so it's thought, and what is more,
It worked. But now it's come to be
A tourist sight of Ottery.
No matter. May its beauty last:
It is a vision of the past.
A crystal circle like a crown,
As sterile waters tumble down.

TRULY THANKFUL

In 1866 a modest book was published called 'Exmouth and its Environs', written by Elizabeth Jane Brabazon. She was a literary lady and she wrote her book after residing in Exmouth at Bastin's Hotel on the Beacon, which she described as 'comfortable'.

Benjamin Butter Bastin kept the Beacon Royal Hotel, and its address was 1 Deacon Hill.

In pursuit of her researches into the neighbourhood the authoress visited Topsham for a short stay in a lodging house kept by a Mrs. 'A'. According to old directories there was at that time a lodging house in Fore Street, Topsham, kept by a Mrs. Adams.

The lodging house was evidently a superior one, as would be expected, but it had at least one serious disadvantage. Nevertheless, whatever the misfortune or calamity, the landlady always found some reason for which to be thankful.

I have translated Elizabeth Jane Brabazon's account of her stay in Topsham into verse form.

Exmouth in 1831 showing Beacon Hill top right.
Engraving by J. Thomas from an original drawing by Thomas Allom.

TRULY THANKFUL

"I'm truly thankful, ma'am," she said,
"For He who watches overhead;
I always thinks that things could be
Much worse—that's my philosophy."

'I'm ever grateful, ma'am, for sure
The Lord will always bring a cure."
Her lodging house looked clean and neat,
A credit to the ancient street.

I thought that Topsham on the Exe
Deserved some study: there were wrecks
Of stricken vessels, history's lore,
It looked to me a treasure store.

She bowed me in and showed me round,
And I was pleased with all I found.
I took two rooms; my stay would be
For two days, or it could be three.

"I'm very grateful, ma'am, I am,
And in the morning there'll be ham
And eggs, and cream, a scrumptious spread.
I knows for sure, you'll like your bed."

And so I did, she was quite right:
I'd rarely spent a better night.
But when I sought my sitting-room,
I coughed and spluttered in the gloom.

A fire was lit, the smoke was thick,
It puffed so much I felt quite sick.
She'd brought my breakfast on a tray:
My ham and eggs looked dark and grey.

Topsham street scene leading down to the Exe Estuary

The landlady came in to see
If all was well. "Lor', gracious me,"
She said, "there is some smoke."
"Some smoke!" I shrieked, "I'm going to choke!"

"I'm truly thankful, ma'am, I am.
(Oh goodness, you have left your ham.)
That chimbley never smokes — at least —
Unless the wind blows from the East."

"For in this life, if things was worse,
It could smeech all the time, perverse."
Next night the wind backed to the North:
Next morning smoke still issued forth.

"Put out the fire, I beg you, please,
With smarting eyes I checked a sneeze.
"This is too bad, and what is clear
To me, in haze, I can't stay here."

She looked at me with sad old eyes,
And poked around to minimize
The gusts of acrid, searing smoke,
Then turned to me, her voice a croak.

"I'm truly thankful, ma'am: God's good.
I must pray harder, that I should,
For that old fire in that old grate
Is something that I've come to hate."

"I'm truly thankful, ma'am," she said
"For He who watches overhead.
But God's been kind, He's always been:
For you'm the first as showed your spleen."

THE DAY TRIP

In the later years of Queen Victoria's long reign a trend began which accelerated for more than a century: more and more people, in widening social groups, began to take holidays by the seaside. There were few thoughts of foreign travel in those times but the coming of the railways had opened up new vistas to the more adventurous and more prosperous. In response to the demand the South Coast resorts in particular developed various attractions, and high on the list of these, along with piers, were paddle steamers.

Pleasure steamers appear to have begun operations in East Devon in 1888 when a firm called Ellett & Matthews of Exmouth purchased a paddle steamer called 'Prince' from Cosens & Company of Weymouth. She was thoroughly overhauled and fitted with a new boiler so that there were no difficulties in passing a Board of Trade survey. There were no piers or jetties on the beaches of Bridport, Seaton, Sidmouth or Budleigh Salterton, so a landing apparatus was devised whereby passengers could be taken aboard and disembarked.

The bows of the ship were slightly cut away and strengthened with iron plates to protect the hull against the harshness of the shingle. As the 'Prince' approached the steeply shelving beaches a stern anchor was dropped. When she grounded the stern anchor rope was hauled tightly enough to hold the vessel bows on the shore. A landing platform, carried aboard, was lowered by tackle. As soon as the Captain gave the 'All Clear', passengers made their way along the contraption, which, endeavouring to be light in weight, was very springy.

Ellett & Matthews prospered and they changed their name to the rather more impressive one of the Devon Streamship Company. It was a proud day for them when they placed an order with the firm of R. & H. Green of Blackwall, London, for a new, steel-built paddle steamer designed with the modifications necessary to negotiate the shelving shingle beaches.

She was named the 'Duchess of Devonshire'. Built in 1891 she was ready to begin service in the summer of 1892. Her length was 170 feet and her gross tonnage was 221. John Penn of Greenwich supplied her compound diagonal two cylinder engines. She proved so successful that the company ordered, from the same makers, and with similar but slightly larger specifications, the 'Duke of Devonshire', delivered in

The 'Duchess of Devonshire' stranded on Sidmouth beach

1896. By 1898 ownership of the two vessels had passed to the Devon Dock, Pier and Steamship Company.

Then an old lady, and after an adventurous life, the 'Duchess of Devonshire' on the 27th August, 1934, came to grief on Sidmouth beach. The rope from the stern anchor broke, she swung round, and was washed broadside on to the shingle. She had to be scrapped on the spot but her remains were there for years until eventually the Council had them removed in 1950.

In this poem a boy describes an excursion in the 'Duchess of Devonshire" in the year 1897.

THE DAY TRIP

Dad had bought the tickets and we stood upon the shingle;
I was so excited that my nerves were all a-tingle.
"Will she come soon?" I asked my Dad. "Oh, quiet, boy," he said.
"Will it be big?" He chuckled. "Not as big as your fat head."
And then I saw her, out at sea, a chrysalis afloat:
A froth of gossamer abeam, a spindrift paddle boat.
"How can we get aboard?" I wailed. "It can't land on this slope."
"I've got the tickets here," said Dad, "the mariners will cope."

And so they did; the paddles threshed and foamed off Sidmouth
                                                          beach.
They lowered a contraption which I thought could never reach.
But it did so and came alive as we began our crossing.
The planks were springy, full of give, an unexpected tossing
Before we'd set to sea. I made it worse by jumping up and down,
Until my father saw me and clipped me with a frown
Across my ear. But I'd had fun and smirked with nasty glee
At frightened looks and girlish screams before we set to sea.

I scampered fast along the deck, all holystoned and white,
I heard Dad's shouts behind me but I was out of sight.
I wanted to explore the ship, to see her inner power,
There wasn't long for we were due at Bridport in an hour.
I saw the cabins down below with seats in russet plush,
The dining room was beautiful, and yet I had to rush
Past startled waiters for I knew that somewhere there must be
The mighty engines, the hot steam, that drove her through the sea.

I stood upon a catwalk, my hands had grasped a rail,
And, lost in awesome wonder, I watched great pistons flail
With spurts of steam, eccentric, and yet with steady beat,
They made their thrusts with juddering power amidst the oily heat.
Then Dad was there beside me. "I knew that you'd be here."
His eyes shone too, for well he knew, I'd be an engineer.
So though the gulls wheeled overhead and as we crossed by Lyme,
My Dad and I were down below amidst the steely grime.

Too soon the voyage ended, we heard the vessel grate
Upon the Dorset pebbles, and Dad and I were late
In climbing the companion-way to join the small array
Of passengers for Bridport who landed at West Bay.
We had some fun, my Dad and me, when we were safe ashore,
Although it clouded over and the wind blew more and more.
We looked out for the 'Duchess' upon her homeward run:
She came on time, and choppy, the boarding was great fun.

And now we stayed upon the deck to watch the foaming sea.
The vessel rolled and pitched a lot as lively as could be;
Our faces glistened with the spray. "Just hang on tight, my lad,"
A sailor called. "I will," I said, and hung on tight to Dad.
The gulls were shrieking at our wake above the good ship's fight.
The paddles shuddered at strange loads, now heavy and now light.
And then the news spread round the boat: it was too rough to land
At Sidmouth. I was scared but glad that I held Father's hand.

"Where shall we go?" I asked my Dad. "Don't worry, son," he said,
"They'll get us back to Sidmouth and you'll sleep in your bed."
We staggered on our way below to have a cup of tea,
But most slopped in the saucer, so lively was the sea.
And then it grew much calmer, and bells rang overhead,
We heard the engines slowing, they lost their measured tread.
We went up to the deck again and I had quite a shock
For we were tied up safely and snug in Exmouth Dock.

The Devon Steamship Company were very, very good,
They took us back to Sidmouth, as Dad said that they would;
They had some wagonettes nearby to take us all that way,
And Dad was pleased because, he said, he didn't have to pay.
It was a long, long creaking ride, a journey in the dark,
I thought that day must dawn quite soon and that I heard a lark.
I told my Dad, he laughed a lot. "We're not too far away,
It's only ten o'clock," he said. It was a lovely day.

A view of West Bay, the old port of Bridport

J. M. W. Turner's watercolour of Sidmouth.
(Reproduction by courtesy of the Whitworth Art Gallery, University of Manchester)

THE KING OF CHET

To the West of Sidmouth are the Chit Rocks. Now low-lying and covered at high tide there was at one time what was then usually called the Chet Rock which stood about forty feet high. It was painted by J. W. Turner, the great English painter, who visited Sidmouth in 1811 and made two sketches of the town and beach.

These he later used in about 1824 for a water colour painting of the town which is now in the Whitworth Art Gallery of the University of Manchester.

It was also reproduced in an engraving in mezzotint with an explanatory text by Ruskin in Turner's 'Harbours of England'. Set in a turbulent sea, a high craggy rock dominates the picture, which is titled 'Sidmouth'.

It has been suggested that the image of the rock, which bears little resemblance to the actual shape of the Chet Rock, was intended as an attack on Lord Sidmouth. To one of radical views, which Turner held, Henry Addington, who became the first Viscount Sidmouth, was an object of hatred and contempt. He had served as Home Secretary and was responsible for some repressive legislation. Probably unfairly, he was held by some to be largely to blame for the infamous Peterloo Massacre.

In 1823 Lord Sidmouth had been the subject of much popular ridicule, a lot of it with bawdy undertones. At the age of sixty-five he had taken as his second wife a much younger woman. Was Turner's portrayal of the rock a lampoon?

Peter Orlando Hutchinson, local historian and man of fine arts, having reached Volume 3 of what was to be his 5-volume 'History of Sidmouth' wrote, in his angular copper-plate, of the Chet Rock as follows:

> 'The Chet-rock stood near the Southern end of the reef. It was about 40 feet high, much beloved by fishermen as on steering in it was the first mark they made. Annually one of them was crowned its king. At low tide he and his court marched out and scrambled to its top where they waved their caps, cheered, and drank to the King of Chet (including the King of England) in smuggled brandy.'

The rock was swept away during the night of the 23rd November, 1824, when a storm of frightening force hit the town.

THE KING OF CHET

I was a king with a kingdom, a kingdom by the sea:
I had my court, I had my crown, I had my fiddlers three.
The dawn had gleamed, the tide had ebbed, when early in the day
We met beside our boats and laughed as cares were blown away.

We had our loads to carry, 'twas brandy for the clerk,
But now 'twas ours, from Branscombe, on donkeys in the dark.
We foot-dragged on the shingle across the Sidmouth strand
Until we reached my kingdom, my own, my native land.

We climbed up forty feet or more, until we reached the turf
Which grew atop my kingdom; we looked down at the surf
Which now, the tide advancing, began to break below
On rocks we knew, yet, truthfully, could never fully know.

The casks were broached, the sun came up, and I was crowned a king:
The King of Chet, the King of Chet, it had a merry ring.
We sang, we laughed, we revelled, it was a holiday.
I wore askew my paper crown, my court around me lay.

They all snored hard, but somehow, I couldn't fall asleep.
I tipped a mug of spirit and downed it good and deep,
Yet even so my pulses raced, my head was bright and clear,
For I was King of Chet, you see, and would be for a year.

The sun moved West, the fisherfolk, my subjects good and true
Began to stir, to slake their thirsts, to look at life anew.
The tide had ebbed, 'twas time to leave, and with a heart-felt song
We praised the day we'd squandered, for working days were long.

We checked our boats from habit before we sought our beds,
We staggered to our loved ones, we laid our tired heads
Upon our cottage pillows, but Margaret had been
Awaiting for the King of Chet, she knew she was his Queen.

But now I've lost my kingdom, my kingdom by the sea:
To be a king was not to be, not for the likes of me.
The Lord saw pride within my heart, and pride's a deadly foe;
The Lord thought hard and thought it right my kingdom had to go.

And so He sent the tempest, the rollers breaking high,
He sent the vicious onslaught that raged from sea and sky;
It was a night of terror, 'twill never be forgot
Until we'm in the churchyard and our flesh begins to rot.

That night was long, I had no sleep, I rowed till I was beat:
I rowed amongst the houses, I rowed down every street,
I saved folks from their windows as did my comrades too,
And all awhile the salt spray stang, the wind it blew and blew.

And when, bemused and tottering, I stood upon the strand,
I looked, and blinked, and sensed a loss: I'd lost my piece of land.
We'd made our mark on Chet for years when coming in to shore
But now, alas, I realised 'twould never be there more.

I was a king with a kingdom, a kingdom by the sea:
I had my court, I had my crown, I had my fiddlers three.
My reign was short for, sadly, my kingdom was upset,
It was my lot, my sorry fate, to be last King of Chet.

The sign of the Volunteer Inn, Broad Street, Ottery St. Mary.
Many such soldiers were to be seen about the town during the Napoleonic Wars.

THE EMIGRATION OF AGNES SALTER

In the early years of the nineteenth century England suffered from the fear of invasion by Napoleon and his victorious armies. Never before had such defensive arrangements been made. In 1803 temporary barracks were built on the lower slopes of West Hill, not far out from Ottery St. Mary, to the left of the road to Exeter. The field where they were situated was later called Barrack Field and Barrack Farm is there to this day. Soldiers were to be seen in the town in droves until the barracks were taken down in 1814.

The Church Marriage Registers show numerous entries of the weddings of local girls to soldiers from other parts of the country. In 1806 there were nearly thirty marriages to soldiers of the Buckinghamshire Militia. An eventual move to Amersham or Aylesbury by a Devon maid who had never travelled more than a few miles from Ottery must have been a more traumatic experience that that of a British G.I. bride moving to the U.S.A. after the last war.

THE EMIGRATION OF AGNES SALTER

I don't know how it happened, but 'twas Springtime on West Hill:
We lay among the bluebells and a faded daffodil
I watch in fixed abandon as he had his way with me.
My eyes were glued upon it in that time of ecstasy.
I knew 'twould upset Mother, and Father, that for sure,
But strangely, as he had me, I felt very, very pure:
For this was true, and we were one. I clutched him in my love.
There was no pain, 'twas beautiful, a gift from heaven above.

I stood up in the bracken, my maidenhead had gone;
I knew I was a woman, and then I looked upon
A sprawling man in uniform, in blue, and red, and gold:
A soldier, yes, a fighter, but not yet very old.
His cheeks were soft and chubby and there was a golden down
Upon his skin, a pollen drift, not culled from any town;
He was a country boy, for sure, though strange, and such is fate,
I couldn't understand his speech, and yet I was his mate.

I took him home to Jesu Street, he asked that he might wed,
He looked so brave and glorious that Father bent his head
As though to give a blessing, while Mother looked so fraught,
And bustled round and made some tea, and said she didn't ought
To interfere when love had bloomed, and Agnes, (that was me),
Had lost her heart, there was no doubt, as all could clearly see;
They didn't want to lose their maid, he'd take her far away,
But he must mind her well, they said, and hand her all his pay.

Then Father talked to Ed, my man: his name was Edwin King,
And told him it was urgent that he bought a wedding ring,
For soldiers came and went, he said, and sometimes had to fight;
For all he knew he might be sent when he got back that night.
I paled at this, and Ma did too, but Eddie shook his head,
"Don't worrit, Mr. Salter, for I'll see that she be wed."
And good as gold he was, my man, he did as he was told,
For on the Sunday of next week in Church our banns were called.

And up above the Barracks in that Springtime on West Hill,
We lay among the flowers and his body was a thrill:
I grew to understand him, although his talk was queer,
And when he held me in his arms he always called me "dear".
In three weeks we were married, four other couples too,
The Church was bright with uniforms of red, and gold, and blue.
And then he went, and me with child; he vowed that he'd return,
"And mind you do," said Mother, "and just send her all you earn."

But Eddie couldn't read or write, though I knew he'd be true,
And so he was, he did his best, he told me what to do:
A note, penned by a friend, arrived, its words were short and clear,
He told me when to catch the coach and I need have no fear.
And what was more, there was some gold, so I could pay the fare,
I was so big with child, yet I knew that I'd get there.
I caught the mail at Fairmile, and Father walked with me,
I clambered to the top, and waved, but Father could not see.

The journey was a nightmare which I never shall forget,
I was told to go to London where he'd told me I'd be met:
I had never been to Exeter or met with city ways,
And here I was in London, so noisy, in a daze
With aching limbs, a headache, and a painful, kicking load,
I managed to set foot again upon a cobbled road.
And there was Ed beside me and I jumped in glad surprise:
He hugged my tired body and he kissed my weeping eyes.

My ordeal was not over, there were many miles to go,
But now that Ed was with me I was in a rosy glow;
This was a strange new world to me I had not visualised,
Except for Eddie's love for me, our baby safe inside.
And now I live near Amersham, they mock my funny speech,
They think I'm very ignorant, Ed's mother tries to teach
Me different ways of doing things, she thinks he married low,
And Ottery I'll never see: that's one thing that I know.

Engraving by P. Heath from an original drawing by W. H. Bartlett published in 1832

THE BELLEROPHON

The extent of the preparations made to resist the invasion of England by Napoleon gives some indication of the awesome fear which he engendered in most of the population.

The imagined young lady who recites this poem would have lived her life under this shadow. The following verse from a lullaby of those times, referring to Napoleon, was unlikely to have allayed childish fears.

> 'And he'll beat you, beat you, beat you,
> Beat you, beat you all to pap.
> And he'll eat you, eat you, eat you,
> Gobble you, gobble you, snap, snap, snap.'

Sidmouth, in Regency times, had become a place of high fashion. Mr. Wallis's Marine Library, mentioned in the poem, was in a central position on the Beach. It was much frequented by upper class visitors and residents.

THE BELLEROPHON

I quivered with excitement when the news came through,
And everything was perfect where we stayed:
We were boarding at the York Hotel, elegant and new,
So convenient for the esplanade parade.
I had never been to Sidmouth, and neither had Mama,
But someone in his club had spoken of it to Papa.
We found the journey tiring as long mile followed mile,
But when at last we reached there we thought it all worthwhile.

It was all so unexpected when the news came through,
And I shivered with excitement at the thought
That the terror of my childhood, laid low at Waterloo,
The Bogeyman of Europe was caught.
And here we were at Sidmouth, and he was in Torbay,
Aboard the 'Bellerophon' not very far away.
I knew I had to see him and I pleaded with Papa,
He wasn't much in favour but he listened to Mama.

Lord Gwydir and Charles Bentinck saw the vessel pass,
They'd watched from Mr. Wallis's that day;
They sat in good society, and looking through a glass,
Were sure they'd seen her anchor far away.
Some wondered whether, really, it was the thing to do,
To take a boat to look at her, and hope to see him too;
I couldn't wait to do so, and lots felt much as me,
So we made up an excursion and early set to sea.

The fishermen of Sidmouth, of Exmouth and Torquay,
Were making lots of money from this trade.
They found it more rewarding than fishing in the sea
As more and more such trips were being made.
They called her 'Billy Ruffian', that stout old man o' war,
She'd fought with Admiral Nelson and many, many more,
At the Battles of Trafalgar, the Nile she'd won fame,
But now she held Napoleon the world would know her name.

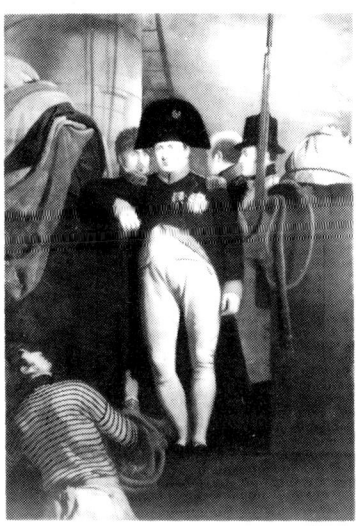

Charles Lock Eastlake's 'Napoleon on Board the Bellerophon' in Plymouth Sound 1815.
Oil on canvas. (Reproduction by courtesy of the National Maritime Museum).

Mama was sniffing smelling salts, Papa was looking queer,
The sea was very choppy on that day;
I quivered with excitement as we began to near
The world's most famous prison in Torbay.
Within a mile of Brixham quay we saw her great bulk loom,
There were hordes of craft around us to see the tyrant's doom;
We tried to pull alongside but this was not allowed
And not surprising, really, considering the crowd.

Our men began to row then, as near as they could go,
And gradually we circled the big ship;
Their sweeps were often clashing and progress was quite slow,
For so many other boats had made the trip.
Papa said I was seeing things, Mama thought much the same,
But behind the high stern windows I saw a little flame
Of sunlight like a halo and just below was he,
The face, now pale and brooding, of sad, dark destiny.

COLLISION AT SEA

In 1862 two Norwegian sailors, B. A. Muller and August Jorgensen were serving on the same vessel as first mate and carpenter respectively. Afterwards their ways parted and they were not to meet again for nearly thirty-two years, and then under violent and tragic circumstances in the English Channel.

The night of the 10th January, 1894, was dark and stormy. Muller, captain of the Norwegian S.S. Edison, a steamer of 289 tons, was bound from Rouen to Cardiff. Jorgensen, now a captain and still serving under sail, was in command of a much larger ship of 794 tons. She was the Norwegian barque, the Ran, battling her way on the long journey from Buenos Aires to Hamburg.

The Edison was steaming at about seven knots, and the Ran, on the look-out for the Portland light, was sailing at a good nine knots. Unknown to them, their only radar the sharpness of the eyes of the crew, they were on collision courses. Suddenly out of the darkness loomed the Edison, crashing into the starboard bow of the Ran. Their position was about thirty-five miles due south of Seaton.

Captain Jorgensen, after some nightmarish moments, found himself, with other members of his crew, on the deck of the sinking steamer. Its boat was launched and when the tally of men aboard was taken all twelve from the steamer were there but of the Ran's complement of fourteen, seven were missing.

Captain Muller, senior man all those years before, took command. It must have been dawn before the two captains recognised each other as old shipmates and possibly long after that. The seas were running high but fortunately the wind was from the south. They had no sail and one of the two oars had been broken in half in the difficult launching. One man steered the boat with a piece of wood, managing to keep her up to the wind, for not until long past daylight, at eleven o'clock the next morning, were they able to get the rudder unshipped. There were no provisions aboard.

During the afternoon they saw three steamers and although they shouted no notice was taken of them. The second engineer of the Edison, Neilson, aged twenty-seven, had succombed to the cold and exposure and appeared to have lost his reason. Darkness fell again over the white-crested seas until at last they saw some lights and frantically pulled towards them.

COLLISION AT SEA

It was snug in the tap on that winter's night,
The flames of the fire were clear and bright,
As they crackled in the grate.
Jim Newton sat with his pipe and his glass,
Not knowing what terror had come to pass,
Caused by a trick of fate.

In the 'Royal Clarence'* by Seaton's shore,
Jim Newton drank, and then ordered more
As his son-in-law came inside.
The wind howled high and the breakers crashed
High on the beach, but their boat was lashed,
Hauled well up from the tide.

Ernest Watts was Jim's son-in-law,
A fisherman, too, and fine and tall,
A comrade good and true.
A word or two dropped from their lips,
They puffed their pipes and took their sips,
'Twas rough out there they knew.

Their ears pricked up, they'd heard a scream:
No gull was this, no waking dream,
For then they heard a cry.
Each took one swig, and then no more,
They rushed from fireside to the door
To find the reason why.

The cold wind cut them like a knife;
They heard more shouts and sounds of strife,
So ran down to the shore.
Though dark they dimly saw a boat,
Amazingly she stayed afloat
Amidst the tempest's roar.

* Now, alas, re-named 'The Sleeper'

A whaling boat she seemed to be,
And as she turned athwart the sea,
A huge wave tossed her down.
She went right over, gunwale smashed,
On foaming shingle she was dashed,
They thought that all must drown.

But then heads bobbed amongst the waves,
And men resisted watery graves
As desperately they fought.
Both Watts and Newton had fetched ropes,
They tried to keep aflame their hopes
Which seemed had come to naught.

The drag of surf an iron bar,
So close inshore and yet so far
From all-inviting land;
With sturdy ropes around them lashed,
Into the waves the two men dashed
To lend a helping hand.

Of nineteen men they saved fifteen,
And three of them were never seen
Again, but one poor soul,
The engineer called Neilsen, stiff
And battered, washed against the cliff
At nearby Seaton Hole.

The captains, shipmates in the past,
Were brought ashore with Muller last,
Jim Newton rescued him.
A roller, savage, knocked them flat,
Jim held him in his grip, and that
Preserved his life and limb.

The folk of Seaton rallied round
With pillows, blankets, quickly found
To warm the frozen men.
The hotel buzzed, the billiard room
Was cleared for them, and dazed by doom
They came to life again.

And hot food nourished, also rum
Began to take effect, so some
Commenced to laugh, set free
From fearsome visions of those nights,
The long, long day, the awesome sights,
The pitching of the sea.

The seven men left aboard the 'Ran'
Released her boat, and they began
To row upon the sound.
Five days had passed before the boat
At Dowlands Cliff was found afloat,
The bodies never found.

The 'Ran', deserted, made her way
To rocks near Chesil Beach, they say,
And finished as a wreck.
A young man thought he ought to do
His very best to save her crew,
And jumped upon her deck.

Though breaking fast, he searched around:
He heard a cry, and then he found
The ship's cat, roaming free.
He got her off and took her home;
For sure she'd never want to roam
Again, or go to sea.

The only body ever found
Was laid to rest in hallowed ground,
A pleasant Devon plot.
In Seaton's churchyard the remains
Of Neilsen rest, the stress and strains
Of his last days forgot.

And Watts' and Newton's bravery
Received rewards for all to see,
With special medals struck.
But best all all, the steamer's boat
Which saved so many, stayed afloat,
And brought Jim Newton luck.

She was repaired and came to be
As fine a craft as put to sea
From Seaton's sloping shore.
And Captain Muller gave to Jim
The boat in gratitude to him,
For no man had braved more.

At Neilsen's inquest, with a tear,
Jorgensen, and in voice sincere,
His gratitude expressed.
The Seaton folk had been so kind,
He'd always keep them in his mind
As people truly blessed.

The Churchyard where Nielsen was buried. The hill from Seaton Church slopes gently downwards towards the River Axe.

OROOLONG

Colyton, with its fourteenth century church crowned by a graceful octagonal tower, its weave of old streets lined by many dignified buildings which indicate the town's prosperous history, always provides a rewarding visit.

As you browse around Colyton you may chance upon an elegant house bearing the unusual name of 'Oroolong House'. You may wonder why it was so called and you may ponder on the intrusion of an obviously foreign word in a setting which is so very English.

'Oroolong' is the name of a small island in that other hemisphere which contains the vast Pacific Ocean. A series of adventures which happened there over two hundred years ago resulted in the publication of a book in 1788 which became a best-seller. It was titled 'An Account of the Pelew Islands ...' and was written by George Keate.

Captain Wilson, the hero of the book, became a celebrity for a short time and was asked to sit for his portrait by Mr. I. Russell, R.A. After his exciting adventures in the Palauan Islands he continued to spend most of his life at sea until he retired to the house in Colyton in 1808. He died on the 10th May, 1810. Many years after his death the gifts which he had received from his South Sea island friends were presented to the British Museum by his relatives.

Colyton Church

OROOLONG

In the August of 1783
The 'Antelope' came to grief:
The packet was in the Philippine Sea
When she hit an uncharted reef.
Under full sail with a following wind
Her timbers ripped with a scream.
The captain knew that his ship was lost:
It seemed like an ugly dream.

Captain Wilson was tough, as were his crew,
And alive to emergency;
All knew exactly what to do,
As they plunged into the sea.
They clung to spars, and the long boat freed,
They loaded aboard what gear
They considered important to help them survive
For this and many a year.

They scrambled ashore at Oroolong,
In the islands of Pelew.
Captain Wilson, brave and strong,
Gave courage to his crew.
For natives armed with spears and shields,
Brown bodies glistening,
Surrounded them, and made no sound:
They stood there, listening.

And Captain Wilson looked around
To see who was their chief.
His searching eyes soon quickly found
The man. To his relief
He recognised nobility
In features bold and fine:
Here was a man of probity,
Son of a royal line.

The two men closed with heads held high,
And stood in front each other;
While piercing eye met piercing eye,
Each recognised a brother.
Then Captain Wilson bowed his head,
As liegeman to his Lord.
They understood, no words were said:
There was complete accord.

The sailors cheered, the natives too,
The high chief grasped the hand
Of Captain Wilson as he threw
His spear upon the sand.
And they they rummaged in the boat
To bring forth wondrous tools;
The chieftain wore the captain's coat,
They danced about like fools.

As time went by there slowly grew
Increasing understanding
Between the natives and the crew
Who, thankful for their landing,
Began to help them in their lives,
And, thanks to Wilson's grip,
He turned their thoughts from native wives
To build themselves a ship.

The chief and Wilson were firm friends:
Without a common tongue
They worked towards their mutual ends
On distant Oroolong.
But while the ship rose on the stocks
Canoes were seen offshore
Threading their way between the rocks
Came tribesmen bent on war.

Now Captain Wilson and his men
Had powder and had shot:
Their guns were quickly loaded, then
They gave them all they'd got.
One man was killed, struck from the skies,
The noise filled them with dread;
They saw white skins and pale blue eyes,
They turned around and fled.

Then Abbu Thulle, the Pelew king,
His foes now far from land,
Removed his heavy chieftain's ring
To place on Wilson's hand.
The natives knelt in homage too,
With wonder in their eyes:
The white man's power they knew was true,
To bring death from the skies.

For years a savage island race
Had raided and caused strife;
They'd fought them off in every case,
Yet always loss of life.
That day a lesson had been taught,
But memories dimmed with time.
When years had passed and wives were sought,
They'd lief repeat their crime.

Wise plans were marked out on the sand,
For Wilson had agreed
To make the raiders understand
They were a conquered breed.
A fleet of war canoes set out,
A Briton sat in each,
The captain led with Abbu Thulle
To storm the alien beach.

The landing with the crash of guns
Struck terror in their hearts;
This killing from a distance was
An unknown martial art.
They gibbered as they ducked in fear,
They grovelled and they squirmed.
That day would never be forgot:
A lesson had been learned.

When back again on Oroolong
All worked upon the boat,
And far too soon for Abbu Thulle
The vessel was afloat.
With rattans for her rigging and
A palm tree for her mast
She looked too frail to venture forth
Upon that ocean vast.

The time had come to say farewell,
To set sail on the sea.
There were sad hearts, for who could tell
What might the future be?
And Abbu Thulle, with open grief,
Grasped Captain Wilson's hand;
Emotions raw, goodbyes were brief,
As they set out from land.

The grateful chief had given them
Some treasures from his store:
The work of craftsmen in the past,
He also gave them more.
He gave his son, a noble Prince,
To Henry Wilson's care.
The Captain failed, could not convince
The Chief to leave him there.

They steered a long and dangerous course
With Wilson at the prow;
He brought his tried and tested force
To safety in Macao.
So Captain Wilson came back home,
He was a man of fame,
For tales were told of what he'd done,
And well-known was his name.

Oroolong House

The prince was feted, honoured, too,
But Oroolong was lost
To him forever, and he knew
In icy death the cost.
And Captain Wilson went to sea,
To storm and hurricane,
Until at last he came back home
To 'Oroolong' again.

THE COACHMAN'S LAMENT

Until the middle of the 18th century the condition of our highways had remained almost without change from medieval times and wheeled vehicles were rare in Devon.

The introduction of turnpike roads and improved methods of road building brought gradual improvements. In 1752 an advertisement in 'The Salisbury Journal' publicised the 'Exeter Fast Coach'. It started every Monday morning from the Saracen's Head, Skinner Street, Snow Hill, London, and in summertime undertook to reach Exeter in 3½ days. It was impossible to travel after dark and the passengers stayed at inns en route. The last leg was from the King's Arms at Dorchester and Exeter was reached at 1 p.m. on the Thursday.

In winter six days were allowed for the journey at an estimated rate of 30 miles a day.

On the 5th February, 1784, the 'Exeter Flying Post' was able to announce: 'the journey to London from Exeter will be accomplished in 32 hours'. On the 2nd August, 1785, mail coaches began to run from London to Exeter and the time had been reduced to 24 hours.

In 1814 the Subscription Coach arrived in Exeter from London in 17 hours.

Not everyone was in favour of these improved road conditions, and many regarded their widening as a waste of land. Some protesters quoted Verse 16 of Chapter 6 of the Book of the Prophet Jeremiah: 'Thus, said the Lord, Stand ye in the ways, and see, and ask for the old paths, where is the good way, and walk therein, and ye shall find rest for your souls'.

This coachman was far from happy in being involved in what was thought to be the march of progress.

THE COACHMAN'S LAMENT

The old paths showed the good way, according to the Lord,
And Jeremiah heard His Voice, and he it was who told
This age-old truth in scriptures writ in aeons long ago:
There would be rest of souls, he said, if we knew where to go.
For I have handled reins for years:
I knew each rutted track.
My stage was safe on that long haul
To Exeter and back.

My father was a coachman, proud born in London town;
And he, like me, drove coaches, and loved to, up and down
To Exeter in springtime, in winter weather too.
The Western road became our lives, and everything we knew.
My father taught me all I know,
But thank God he has died,
For if, today, he held the reins,
He would be terrified.

For there have come the turnpikes, our masters had to pay,
And what that meant to coachmen was far more miles each day.
We earned no more, and, what was worse, with roads so hard
                                                    and true,
The horses became careless, and sometimes we did too.
We missed the grip of those old tracks,
As speed became the aim.
McAdam did no good for us,
Despite his growing fame.

My life has come to be too fast: I'm now a slave to clocks.
Gone are the free and easy ways, for then a coachman's box
Was his command, a proud place, my skills had earned renown,
And when I drove to Exeter and back again to town
I never risked my passengers,
I kept a steady pace;
Though time was never wasted,
We did not run a race.

This engraving by J. F. Lambert from an original drawing by W. H. Bartlett was published in 1832. The New London Inn was built on the site of the old Oxford Inn. For several years before and subsequent to 1830 the stables of most of the inns in Exeter were crowded with horses. In the stables of the New London Inn there were kept not less than 350 horses.

I knew each tricky piece of road, I had to concentrate,
It did not really matter if at times we came in late.
And when, as night began to fall, I wheeled on cobbled stones,
I knew there would be food and drink to solace tired bones.
They always made us welcome,
And I had friends galore
In those old inns along our route;
No man could ask for more.

But now it's faster, faster: my master cracks the whip,
And I am in a lather in case my horses trip.
In my old age it's clear to me that I can't stand the speed.
Is life so short, I wonder, that there should be this need
For changing teams in seconds,
Of such frenetic haste?
The irony — I'm growing old.
There is less time to waste.

The Book of Jeremiah spoke truth, of that I'm sure,
There was wisdom in the old ways, when life was more secure,
And dignified, and civilized, and sensible as well —
We are trotting on a frenzied path that's leading straight to Hell.
For what is speed? I ask myself.
Life cannot be a waste
If there is time to savour it,
To get to know its taste.

THERE'S BRIMSTONE IN MY NOSTRILS

Although there were similar traditions in other East Devon towns, and, indeed, in other parts of England, it is remarkable that the ancient fire festival which takes place on the 5th November in Ottery St. Mary has continued in its long established and rather frightening way. Dawn is blasted by shattering explosions caused by what are called 'rock cannons', old devices which, it mishandled, can cause the loss of a limb. During the day there is a growing excitement which, possibly, only Ottregians can fully savour.

When darkness comes there is a carnival procession. This is a popular entertainment in East Devon and various firms and organisations vie with each other in pouring tremendous energy into providing colourful and animated floats lit by myriads of electric light bulbs powered by towed generators which add a low buzz to the tinny, reverberating blasts from the hightly decibelled speakers.

Then there is a bonfire near St. Saviour's Bridge. It seems to grow bigger each year, sending its sparks into the sky and illuminating the old factory, late eighteenth century, but now adjusted to modern technology. Not so many years ago there had been a spell of dry weather so prolonged that people were able to sit on the grassy banks watching the towering flames. Just imagine, in November. There is always a thrill when there is some unusual spectacle and so there was on that occasion: it was a never-to-be-forgotten sight, that of little groups sitting, their faces lit by the flames, their dry bottoms defying Nature's normal laws.

The climax of the evening is the dangerous practice of the 'rolling of the tar barrels'. It is not easy to find barrels these days but somehow they are provided in Ottery. Soaked in tar, and open-ended,. they are ignited and carried on the shoulders of young men who run amongst the dense crowds.

One such young man describes his experience.

THERE'S BRIMSTONE IN MY NOSTRILS

There's brimstone in my nostrils, there's fire in the night,
There's coals inside my belly, and my blood is all alight;
I've been drinking in the Lamb and Flag, and in the London too,
But all the flames inside me are not from any brew.
The spark was lit in Ottery so many years ago
When first I learned the barrelling in Paternoster Row.
My father told me what to do, Grandpa had taught him too,
There were few words yet, somehow, I knew just what to do.
> Shatter the dawn with crackers,
> Start with a cannonade:
> For we are the attackers,
> Bent on a fiery raid.

Although November days are short, today's been very long
With waiting for the sun to set, so we could get among
The shadows and the dimpsy* where a flame can make its mark,
For fire is paled by daylight, but when it's getting dark
It roars into magnificence, its hold is then supreme,
It is a weird and vivid force inside a waking dream.
I can't explain my feelings, and neither could my Dad;
I know I have to do it, although I must be mad.
> May I not flinch when I lift it,
> May I not falter nor fail;
> Give me the strength to shift it,
> Blazing a fiery trail.

I'm getting more excited as the crowds begin to surge,
I'm donning dampened clothing, as now I feel the urge
To prove a point of manhood as my forbears did before.
We don't know how this started but there is ancient lore
This was a heathen custom before we had our Church.
We turned it to our Christian ways and so we could besmirch
The poor old Pope by burning him when Henry wanted wives.
For centuries we've done it: a custom that survives.
> Let me get into the masses,
> Let me see wonder and fear
> Flushing the faces of lassies,
> Bringing a fiery cheer.

* dimpsy — dialect word meaning 'twilight'

62

The boys' barrel

The barrel's on my shoulders and the flames are burning hot,
I'm running like a rabbit with a fear of being shot.
The crowds are shrieking "Oohs" and "Ahs" and screeching as
I chase;
They are a blur but now and then I note a pretty face
With open eyes lit up with fear, her rosy cheeks aglow
From the fire that I carry as through the press I go.
There is no space, give me a chance, don't form a human bar;
They scatter as I rush at them ablaze with hissing tar.
　　　I've never been quite so excited,
　　　I've never had power like this,
　　　I am like a being benighted:
　　　I'm lost in a fiery bliss.

I've run like this for centuries, I feel it in my bones:
These are old pagan forces with darker undertones.
And I'm as brave and brave can be, I've proved it so to all,
Although I'm crouched while running, I'm feeling very tall;
I'm panting now, a cloud of steam, my hands are wet with heat,
My shoulders burn, my head's afire, and yet I won't be beat.
I carry on, my breath in sobs, then there's a mighty crack:
The barrel's burst, a star shell, and the load's gone from my back.

    So now I can drink to my manhood.
    And drink deep into the night.
    For I've fought the flames as a man should:
    I've won the fiery fight.